EXTREME SCIENTISTS™

DIGGING UP HISTORY: ARCHAEOLOGISTS

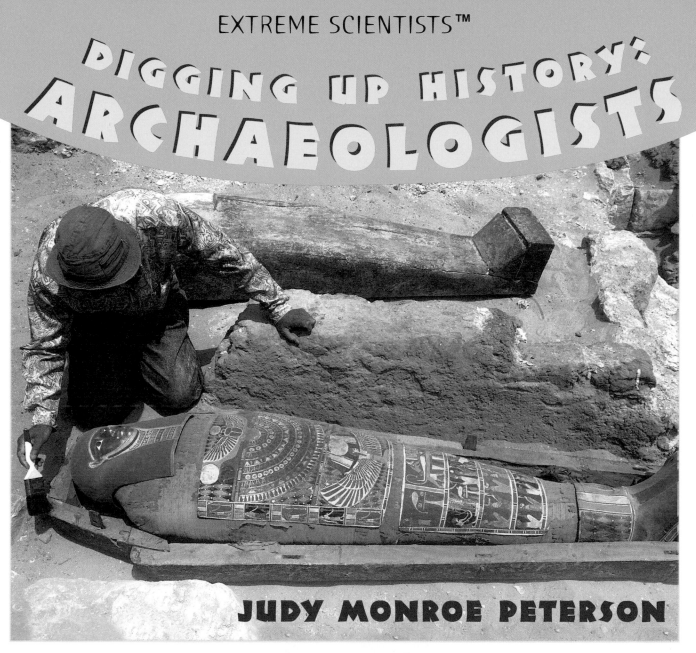

JUDY MONROE PETERSON

PowerKiDS
press™
New York

To Alex, Ayla, and Anthony

Published in 2009 by The Rosen Publishing Group, Inc.
29 East 21st Street, New York, NY 10010

First Edition

Editor: Amelie von Zumbusch
Book Design: Kate Laczynski
Photo Researcher: Jessica Gerweck

Photo Credits: Cover, pp. 1, 9, 13, 17 © AFP/Getty Images, Inc.; pp. 5, 19 © National Geographic/Getty Images; pp. 7, 15 Shutterstock.com; p. 11 © WireImage/Getty Images; p. 21 © Superstock.com.

Library of Congress Cataloging-in-Publication Data

Peterson, Judy Monroe.
  Digging up history : archaeologists / Judy Monroe Peterson. — 1st ed.
     p. cm. — (Extreme scientists)
  Includes index.
  ISBN 978-1-4042-4523-5 (library binding)
 1. Archaeologists—Juvenile literature. 2. Archaeology—Juvenile literature. 3. Antiquities—Juvenile literature.
4. Excavations (Archaeology)—Juvenile literature. I. Title.
  CC107.P47 2009
  930.1—dc22

                           2008006837

Manufactured in the United States of America

CONTENTS

Clues to the Past

Are you interested in how people lived thousands of years ago? If you are, you might like to work as an **archaeologist**. Archaeologists are scientists who study how people lived in the past. They learn about ancient, or very old, people by finding and studying artifacts. An artifact is any object made or used by a person.

Tools, clothing, and pictures are artifacts. Bricks from a house and cooking pots are artifacts, too. Rocks, sticks, and bones that people used to hunt or to prepare food are also artifacts. Archaeologists use artifacts to piece together facts about the past and tell the story of how people lived long ago.

This archaeologist is studying a Maya artifact. The Mayas lived in Mexico and Central America. They founded cities and invented advanced math and writing systems.

In the Ground

Archaeologists study artifacts from many kinds of sites. Sites are places where people lived and left remains. Some sites are places people buried trash. Other sites are places dead people were buried with special objects. Some large sites are whole towns that were covered by sand, **ash**, or mud.

One well-known site is the Cahokia Mounds, along the Mississippi River in Illinois. Cahokia was governed by strong rulers. Hundreds of years ago, as many as 20,000 people lived there. Today, archaeologists are digging up Cahokia's 1,000-year-old trash pits and buried houses.

DID YOU KNOW?

The people of Cahokia lived in houses built in rows around a large, central square. The people ate corn, beans, squash, and nuts and enjoyed songs, dances, and games.

Machu Picchu, in what is now Peru, is a well-known archaeological site. The Incas built this city high in the Andes Mountains.

Finding Sites

Sometimes, archaeologists find sites by chance. **Construction** workers find artifacts when digging in the ground. Farmers pick up old coins or tools when **plowing**. People spot parts of old buildings from planes, too. These clues show where more artifacts might be found. Archaeologists find other sites by looking for them. Archaeologists know where to look because they read maps or old papers to discover where people once lived.

Once archaeologists have found a site, they do a survey, or study, of it. Archaeologists often dig evenly spaced holes in the ground and study what they find there. This helps them guess them where to look for more artifacts.

In 1974, Chinese farmers who were digging a well discovered more than 6,000 clay soldiers buried with an early Chinese ruler.

Exploring Tombs

Some archaeological sites are tombs. A tomb is a place where one or more dead people are buried. Sometimes, tombs have special objects in them for the people buried there to use in the **afterlife**. These objects give us clues about what ancient people believed.

In 1922, British archaeologist Howard Carter discovered the tomb of Tutankhamen, a king who ruled Egypt more than 3,000 years ago. The young king was buried with 5,000 artifacts, such as gold, **jewels**, furniture, **weapons**, and clothing. He also had games and models of food, boats, and animals.

DID YOU KNOW?

In the late 1920s, British archaeologist C. Leonard Woolley discovered the royal tombs at Ur, in today's Iraq. Here, ancient Sumerians were buried with riches of gold, silver, and jewels.

This gold artifact from Tutankhamen's tomb held the dead king's inner organs, or inside body parts.

Underwater Sites

Sometimes, archaeologists find sites under water. Some underwater sites are ships that sank. Towns and cities that were flooded by the ocean are also underwater sites. To find underwater sites, archaeologists use a tool called sonar. Sonar sends sound waves toward the ocean floor. The waves spring back when they hit something and show where underwater objects are.

In 1978, archaeologists began studying the *San Juan*, a Spanish ship that sank in Red Bay, Canada, in 1565. The sailors on the *San Juan* hunted whales, as oil made from whale fat was used for heat and light at that time.

DID YOU KNOW?

In 1912, the RMS *Titanic* sank after hitting an iceberg. Archaeologists have found leather, metal, and clay objects from the people on this mighty ship. They even discovered letters in mail sacks!

This archaeologist is studying a ship that sank in the Mediterranean Sea near the town of Kas in Turkey.

Uncovering Lost Cities

Lost cities are among the largest archaeological sites. The cities that the Mayas built between A.D. 300 and A.D. 900 were once lost in the forests of Mexico, Guatemala, Belize, and Honduras. The Mayas built large **pyramids** and invented calendars and writing. Archaeologists have found cloth, clay pots, and gold at Maya sites.

In A.D. 79, Mount Vesuvius, in Italy, blew up and hot stones and ash buried the nearby city of Pompeii. Today, archaeologists have partly uncovered Pompeii. They found beautiful wall paintings that show daily life in ancient Pompeii. These and other artifacts showed archaeologists that the people of Pompeii enjoyed music and kept clean at large public baths.

Visitors to Pompeii can walk down ancient paved streets and see the remains of buildings that are thousands of years old.

Discovering Artifacts

When working on a site, archaeologists are very careful. They dig with small shovels and tools called trowels. They take dirt from the site and pile it on **screens**. Then they shake the dirt off to uncover artifacts. The archaeologists clean dirt from artifacts with toothbrushes. Sometimes, they use tools called metal detectors that sense metal objects to find hidden artifacts.

Archaeologists note where each artifact is found and what is nearby. They measure and record the position and depth of each artifact. The archaeologists also take pictures of every artifact. They save all the pictures and facts on computers.

This archaeologist is carefully removing the dirt from a mosaic, or picture made of pieces of tile, in Bordeaux, France.

Working in a Lab

Archaeologists take some of the artifacts they find at sites to study in labs. Labs are full of tools that archaeologists can use to study artifacts. For example, carbon-14 dating tools tell the age of artifacts. Archaeologists use tools called microscopes to look closely at bone pieces, seeds, and **pollen**. What they learn helps scientists describe what the weather was like in the past.

X-ray machines and other special tools measure the size and shape of artifacts. Archaeologists also use argon plasma spectrometers, tools that find **elements** that tell where and when metal artifacts were made.

DID YOU KNOW?

Archaeologists also use a method called mass spectrometry to study artifacts. In 2007, they used it to discover that seeds found in floors of ancient Peruvian houses were 10,000 years old!

Archaeologists in labs use many tools to study mummies. Mummies are the bodies of dead people that have been preserved, or kept from rotting.

19

Ancient Languages

Sometimes, archaeologists find artifacts with ancient writing on them. This writing can be hard to read because it often uses languages or writing systems that are not used today. One such writing system is **cuneiform**. The Sumerians began writing in cuneiform more than 5,000 years ago.

Around that time, Egyptians began to use **hieroglyphics**. By A.D. 300, people had stopped using hieroglyphics. Early archaeologists could not read hieroglyphics found at Egyptian sites. In 1799, the Rosetta Stone, a stone with a message written in hieroglyphics and two other writing systems, was discovered in Egypt. In 1822, Jean-François Champollion used this stone to figure out how to read hieroglyphics.

The walls of the tomb of Egyptian ruler Ramses VI are covered with hieroglyphics. Ramses VI ruled Egypt from 1145 to 1137 B.C.

Becoming an Archaeologist

Most archaeologists have studied for many years. They need to know math, science, and history. Young archaeologists also learn many skills by working in labs or digging at sites.

If you are interested in archaeology, there are many ways to learn more. Ask science **museums** about their youth archaeology camps. In these camps, kids study artifacts and work at archaeological sites. Look in newspapers to see when archaeologists are giving talks about their work or tours of their sites. Visit museums and artifact collections on the Internet or in person. You may discover that learning about the lives of people from the past is in your future.

GLOSSARY

afterlife (AF-ter-lyf) Where people believe they will go after they die.

archaeologist (ahr-kee-AH-luh-jist) Someone who studies the remains of peoples from the past to understand how they lived.

ash (ASH) Pieces of tiny rock that shoot out of a volcano when it blows.

construction (kun-STRUK-shun) Having to do with building.

cuneiform (kyoo-NEE-uh-form) Old writing made up of narrow triangular shapes.

elements (EH-luh-ments) The basic matter of which all things are made.

hieroglyphics (hy-eh-ruh-GLIH-fiks) A form of writing that uses more than 700 pictures for different words and sounds.

jewels (JOO-elz) Highly valued stones.

museums (myoo-ZEE-umz) Places where art or historical pieces are safely kept for people to see and to study.

plowing (PLOW-ing) Using a machine to cut, lift, and turn over soil.

pollen (PAH-lin) A dust made by the male parts of flowers.

pyramids (PEER-uh-midz) Large, stone forms with a square bottom and triangular sides that meet at a point on top.

screens (SKREENZ) Fine netting through which very little can pass.

weapons (WEH-punz) Objects used to hurt or kill.

Due to the changing nature of Internet links, PowerKids Press has developed an online list of Web sites related to the subject of this book. This site is updated regularly. Please use this link to access the list:
www.powerkidslinks.com/exsci/archae/